CHRISTIAN VIII
King first of Norway
and then of Denmark

by Jens Gunni Busck

Historika

Published in cooperation with the Royal Danish Collection

CONTENTS

Table clock in gilded bronze featuring a statuette of Christian VIII sitting at a table in uniform. This fine clock was made by the firm A & W Jacobsen.

KING IN A GOLDEN AGE

It is surely unusual for a king to do greater things than those for which he is remembered, but this can be said of Christian VIII (1786–1848). As the first constitutional king of Norway and the last absolute monarch of Denmark, he bore his share of the responsibility for the creation of both the Norwegian and the Danish constitutions, but for various reasons, the space accorded him in history books is modest in both countries. However, Christian VIII was a king with unusual abilities and whose story bears witness to the great political dilemma of the age: that the need for democratic reforms constantly became more urgent but threatened the existing order.

Christian Frederik portrayed by Amélie Romilly in Geneva, 1821.

In Denmark, the first half of the nineteenth century is called the Golden Age because of the many outstanding artists, poets, and thinkers who lived during the period and paid visits to Amalienborg in a steady stream. Until 1839, however, it was not the palace of the king that attracted them, for the king at the time, Frederik VI, had very limited interest in talking with such individuals. Rather, it was the King's cousin and successor, Prince Christian Frederik, across the square, who was practically intoxicated by art, literature, and science throughout his life. If there was a King of the Danish Golden Age, then it was this man, who became Christian VIII after the death of Frederik VI. But of course it was not as a patron of the arts, a collector, or an amateur scientist that he made his most important contribution, but as a political actor at the end of the age of absolute monarchy.

The young Christian Frederik received his baptism of fire in 1814 when, as the governor of Norway, he mobilized the Norwegians to fight for their independence after Denmark had been forced to hand over Norway to Sweden as a result of the Napoleonic wars. This led to the adoption of the Constitution of Norway, which was one of the most progressive constitutions in Europe at that time. As a consequence of Sweden's military superiority, Christian Frederik was forced to abdicate and leave Norway after only a few months as a constitutional king, but he managed to save the constitution so Norway avoided becoming a Swedish province.

The mature Christian VIII took his place on the Danish throne in 1839 in the context of an entirely different situation in which liberal tendencies were making waves, but both domestic and international political considerations made it necessary to proceed much more carefully. In Denmark, ruling became a balancing act; and while he knew that the absolute monarchy would have to make way for a constitutional system when the time was ripe, Christian VIII did not live long enough to introduce a new constitution in Denmark.

There is no doubt that Christian VIII is among the most gifted kings Denmark and Norway have had, but despite the facts that his extant letters, diaries, and records are extensive, it is very difficult to gain a good understanding of his simultaneously emotional and distanced elegance. There is also a special question associated with this king that is impossible to answer, namely, to what extent people around him knew that from a biological point of view, he had nothing to do with the Norwegian or Danish throne.

Officially an Oldenburger

Prince Christian Frederik was born at Christiansborg on 18 September 1786 as the eldest son of Hereditary Prince Frederik and Princess Sophie Frederikke of Mecklenburg-Schwerin. After nearly twelve years of childless marriage, this was of course a joyous occasion, and the joy was not diminished when the couple produced two daughters and another son during the following years. The sudden onset of fertility was not entirely miraculous, however, for all the evidence indicates that the perpetuation of the Oldenburg line was left to the Hereditary Prince's adjutant, Frederik von Blücher. One indication that the Hereditary Prince was not the father of Christian Frederik and his siblings is that the children showed no sign of the underbite that characterized the ruling family.

Christian Frederik's mother, Princess Sophie Frederikke, was an intelligent and lively lady who is said to have been fonder of her children than of her husband. She died of pneumonia when Christian Frederik was eight years old, and some have emphasized this sudden loss of maternal care as an explanation of the fact

that the prince built up an impenetrable facade of affable charm but had difficulty establishing deep emotional connections with others. It might be yet more justifiable to see a causative relationship between his mother's early death and the constant need for erotic distraction that characterized his life as an adult.

Christian Frederik does not seem to have had a close relationship with his official father, but it was to his advantage that the Hereditary Prince was able to create

Christian VIII's mother, Hereditary Princess Sophie Frederikke, portrayed by Jens Juel in the early 1790s.

The first Christiansborg was a sumptuous prestige building erected by Christian VI in the 1730s. On 26 February 1794, the palace burned, and the fire had broken out in precisely those rooms in which Christian Frederik lived, though the fire was not his fault. This was a national catastrophe, where a tremendous number of valuable objects were lost, and the fire rendered the royal family homeless, which resulted in the royal takeover of Amalienborg. The picture was painted the same year by C. D. Fritzsch, who had witnessed the fire.

an intellectually stimulating environment in Christian Frederik's home at Amalienborg. From an early age, Christian Frederik learned to converse with the foremost artists, writers, and professors of his age, and he continued to do so all his life.

Christian Frederik's upbringing was planned by the Hereditary Prince and his old friend, Ove Høegh-Guldberg, and undertaken in Christian Frederik's home

by highly qualified teachers. Christian Frederik's schooling was comprehensive and characterized by a balance between the humanistic subjects and the natural sciences. The legacy of classical antiquity was emphasized, and training of his stylistic and rhetorical abilities clearly benefited the prince later in life. In accordance with Høegh-Guldberg's instructions, Christian Frederik received his schooling alone, as intercourse with schoolmates could lead to unhealthy impulses.

It must be said that the prince had been born into a somewhat-complicated royal familial situation. Since 1766, Christian VII had nominally been King, but he was not capable of ruling. During the years 1770–1772, the man who in fact governed was the King's highly controversial personal physician, J. F. Struensee; and after Struensee lost his head in 1772, the Queen Dowager, Juliane Marie, and her son, Frederik, the Hereditary Prince, were the real heads of state, while Høegh-Guldberg provided important support. This changed with the coup of 1784 when Crown Prince Frederik (VI) and a circle around him dissolved the Council of State and seized governmental power. With this, the Crown Prince cut off his maternal grandmother (the Queen Dowager) and his uncle (the Hereditary Prince) from influence, so relations between the two branches of the family were cold when Christian Frederik was growing up.

At his confirmation in 1803, however, the entire royal family came together, and here Christian Frederik got his first opportunity to impress people with his amazing talent for public speaking. After this, he was treated like an adult, and he also received friendly attention from Crown Prince Frederik, who, having lost two sons himself, understood that it was entirely possible that the young prince would succeed him as King.

As part of their education, royals of that age were expected to undergo artistic training; and as in all other areas, Christian Frederik turned out to be an exemplary pupil in this regard. He received training at the Royal Danish Academy of Fine Arts in the late 1790s, and this picture of a boy is probably from 1798 when the Prince was twelve years old.

A matrimonial drama

The year Christian Frederik was confirmed, he accompanied the Hereditary Prince on a lengthy journey to Germany. During a stay at the palace of Ludwigslust, which was the home of the family of the Duke of Mecklenburg, the prince met his cousin Princess Charlotte Frederikke, who was two years older than he was, and he was as if bewitched. Of his departure, he wrote in his diary that "as long as we drove I was unable to stop crying," which was characteristic of both

Portrait of Princess Charlotte Frederikke painted by F. C. Gröger probably between 1804 and 1806. Throughout her life, the unstable but certainly not boring Charlotte Frederikke succeeded in giving the people around her something to talk about. In 1829, after many years of exile in Horsens, she moved to Rome, where she befriended many, including Bertel Thorvaldsen. She was never able to become reacquainted with her son "Fritz" and died in Rome in 1840.

the prince and his time. Sentimentality was not only accepted but cultivated, and it was not considered problematic for men to be seen crying.

While the time of strictly arranged marriages was over, those closest to Christian Frederik tried to get him to change his mind, for it was the family's wish that he would marry Crown Prince Frederik's eldest daughter in order to patch over the quarrel between the two branches of the family. Also, others had better eyes for the chosen cousin's weaknesses; she was emotionally unstable and in fact unsuitable for taking on a prominent position at the court.

After a further visit to the Duke's family in 1804, the prince's family had to give in to the wishes of the young pair. But for the time being, the wedding was postponed due to the prince's youth. According to a folk belief, the reason for the postponement was that Charlotte Frederikke became pregnant and the following year gave birth to the later-famous Miss (Jomfru) Fanny, who lived in Aabenraa and was supposed to be a seer, but this was disproved long ago.

During the fall of 1805, Christian Frederik became seriously involved with the army—as princes were supposed to—and served in Holstein. Military life bored him, but he was glad to have the company of his beloved after the couple had been married at a modest wedding at Ludwigslust in the summer of 1806. The marriage got off to a poor start, however, for in the spring of 1807, Charlotte Frederikke bore a son that died immediately after birth. Sometime after this, the young couple got permission to move to Copenhagen, where the princess gave birth to another son, Prince Frederik (VII), on 6 October 1807. But by this point, the marriage was already in a serious crisis. In his letters, Christian Frederik complained of his wife's uncontrolled fits of rage and inappropriate attempts to make him jealous, which could well have had to do with the sexual infidelity of which she could have had good reason for suspecting him. In 1809, things got to be too much for Frederik VI after it had become generally known that Charlotte Frederikke was having an affair with her singing teacher. The King had her banished, first to Altona in Germany and then to Horsens.

Portrait of Prince Frederik (VII) as a child. The artist is unknown, but the picture is believed to be one of a series of portraits that were painted for the Prince's mother, Princess Charlotte Frederikke, so that she would be able to follow her son's growth from her exile in Horsens.

The wrecked marriage was a major defeat for Christian Frederik, who had experienced nothing but applause in his life up to this point. Naturally, the course of

The Gala Hall in the former Levetzau's Palace at Amalienborg, which was later renamed Christian VIII's Palace. After taking over the palace in 1794, Frederik, the Hereditary Prince, had it magnificently restored. The artist Nicolai Abildgaard was responsible for the interiors in most of the palace. The Gala Hall was decorated with two statues of goddesses executed by a very young Bertel Thorvaldsen, who was apprenticed to Abildgaard. Christian Frederik took over the palace when the Hereditary Prince died in 1808.

For better or worse, Christian VIII's life was marked by his relationship to his predecessor, Frederik VI (1768–1839), who ruled Denmark for more than half a century—from 1784 until 1808 as Crown Prince and from 1808 until his death as King. The two "cousins" were not in agreement politically, and in general, they could not have been more different. While Frederik VI was ascetic and oriented towards military matters, Christian VIII was a decided civilian who appreciated fine cuisine and possessed a highly developed sense of art and culture that Frederik VI lacked. However, their correspondence indicates that for the most part, they got along well. Portrait by F. C. Gröger, 1808.

events was also unpleasant for the Princess, who was forced to leave her son. She had married a highly self-absorbed young man who was probably mostly in love with his own being in love and was unable to confront the personality disorder from which she may have suffered.

The road to Norway

While these private problems were ongoing, dramatic events were taking place in Denmark-Norway, both with regard to the military and the political situations. In 1801, large parts of the Danish-Norwegian fleet had been annihilated at the Battle of Copenhagen, and the policy of neutrality to which Crown Prince Frederik (VI) returned during the following years turned out to be impossible to maintain. Napoleon's superior war machine rolled across Europe, and in 1807, England demanded the handing over of the Danish fleet, which resulted in the Second Battle of Copenhagen (Bombardment of Copenhagen) in September of the same year. In the context of this background, Denmark-Norway concluded an alliance with Napoleon that was also supposed to serve as a buttress against Sweden, where the old dream of swallowing up Norway—which was geographically understandable—lived on. The alliance made it necessary to declare war on Sweden in 1808; Frederik VI hoped to reconquer the areas that had been lost to Sweden in the seventeenth century, while Sweden hoped to take Norway. Neither side's hope was realized.

For Christian Frederik, Norway, which had been under the Danish crown since 1536, constituted an area of special interest. In 1806, he took over the Hereditary Prince's role as head of the Royal Norwegian Society of Sciences and Letters. While this was only an honorary position, the Prince put his heart and soul into fulfilling the responsibilities associated with it. This gave him a reason to keep himself informed with regard to conditions in Norway, and his efforts were supported by his friendship with the Norwegian Carsten Anker, who had visited Christian Frederik's home at Amalienborg during the Hereditary Prince's time.

In 1811, it was decided that Norway should have its own university; and when a festival was held in Copenhagen for this reason, Christian Frederik got an opportunity to impress the governmental elite with a bombastic, florid speech—just the kind of thing people preferred during that age. While he still stood out-

Christian Frederik in the uniform of Frederik VI's life regiment. Pastel portrait by Christian Hornemann, 1810.

side the circles of power, this helped to establish his credentials as Norway's man in Copenhagen.

Christian Frederik was in fact briefly also in play as a possible successor to the Swedish throne. In 1809, the Swedish king kong Gustav IV Adolf was removed via a coup d'état, and Karl XIII was installed in his place. This made possible the conclusion of a peace treaty between Denmark-Norway and Sweden, but there was a lack of a successor, as the new King was elderly and childless. Prince

Already during his journey to Germany in 1803, Christian Frederik had his first meeting with Napoleon's self-confident army commander, Jean-Baptiste Bernadotte (1763–1844), who, as Sweden's Crown Prince, would become the most important political opponent in his life. This is a portrait of Bernadotte by François Gérard painted in 1811, shortly after he had become the successor to the Swedish throne and taken the name Charles John (Karl Johan).

Christian August of Augustenborg was chosen but died the following year, and Christian Frederik was now discussed as a candidate in Swedish circles that would have liked to have seen the Nordic countries united under a single throne. However, this was rendered impossible by the fact that Frederik VI, in a fairly unrealistic fashion, proposed himself as a candidate for the second time, which prevented Christian Frederik from promoting himself. Given the lack of better options (and because he was able to offer the Swedish state a large loan at a low rate of interest), it was Napoleon's well-known marshal, the Frenchman Jean-Baptiste Bernadotte, who became the successor to the Swedish throne, taking the name Karl Johan (Charles John).

The choice of Bernadotte meant that a unification of Sweden and Norway would not be implemented by peaceful means, for the main point on his agenda was conquering Norway. In 1811, Karl Johan sought support for this from Napoleon, but he was refused assistance by Napoleon, and this caused him instead to offer Russia his help against Napoleon, in return for Russian help conquering Norway. Agreement was reached in April 1812, and when Napoleon's army was almost destroyed later the same year during the campaign against Russia, it became clear that Denmark had made a bad move when it had aligned itself with France. Christian Frederik had long spoken in favour of an alignment with England, but Frederik VI continued to maintain the alliance with Napoleon and only sent diplomats to England when it was too late.

In March 1813, Karl Johan succeeded in convincing England to become a party to the Swedish-Russian agreement, and the following month he broke off diplomatic relations with Denmark-Norway. Shortly thereafter, in late April, Christian Frederik got what he had long wished for: he was sent to Norway as governor.

The king of revolt

The journey to Norway was carefully camouflaged. It was officially announced that Christian Frederik would now be a general in Holstein, so he first travelled to Als and then incognito through Jutland. Disguised as a sailor, the prince departed from Frederikshavn on a fishing boat. It was considered given that Christian Frederik's mission would be to secure Norway's independence, and all the involved parties—including ordinary Norwegians—understood this to be the

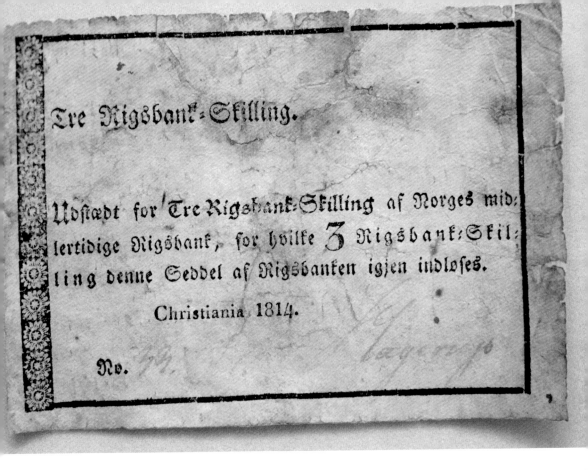

case. The following year and a half was a decisive time both for the prince and for Norway.

Governor

Christian Frederik was received as a hero when he rode into Christiania (Oslo) on 22 May 1813. Although the prince was quite fond of applause, one might imagine that he was not entirely comfortable in this situation. He had no real military experience to help him if there should be a war, and his administrative experience was limited to what he had obtained in connection with holding the relatively undemanding position of head—a kind of board chairman—of the Royal Danish Academy of Fine Arts in Copenhagen, which he had held since 1809. His Norwegian staff was small, he knew none of his potential advisors and helpers,

Christian Frederik's Norwegian royal signet with Norway's coat of arms enclosed by the collar of the Order of the Elephant. Signet ring of agate mounted on gilded silver, made in England in 1814.

and correspondence with Copenhagen was slow. On the other hand, Christian Frederik had been given a great deal of freedom to act as he saw fit by his instructions from Frederik VI, and he would exploit this freedom.

In the beginning, he needed to establish a foothold and secure support. The new governor was invited to many social events, of course, and he attended as many of these as he could manage to. But at the same time, a huge number of extant letters and memoranda bear witness to the unusual capacity for work that Christian Frederik now got his first opportunity to manifest.

It was also decisive to get the country sufficient supplies of grain, for when Christian Frederik arrived, Norway was on the verge of famine, which was largely due to the fact that grain transports by sea had been blocked by the English navy. Naturally, this had been brought about by the Swedish crown prince Karl Johan, as starvation was a useful tool to ensure submission to Sverige. The problem was alleviated by transferring responsibility for the grain trade to private importers who found other transport routes.

Several times in the course of 1813, Frederik VI gave Christian Frederik direct orders to attack Sweden, but he refused because the condition of the Norwegian army was too poor. Sweden did not invade Norway immediately because the great powers demanded that Sweden first make a contribution to the final confrontation with Napoleon. To be sure, Russia had withdrawn its support for an attack on Norway, but England was willing to support such an attack in return for Swedish participation in the war against Napoleon.

This participation was unpleasant for Sweden's Crown Prince, for he was not eager to make war on his own countrymen, and he managed to avoid having to fight in French territory. But once he had fulfilled his obligations to the alliance, Karl Johan immediately began to prepare to attack Denmark from the south. On 7 December 1813, the first engagements with Danish forces in Holstein took place; and while the great powers were significantly misinformed with regard to the Swedish advance, the Danish defences were overwhelmed so quickly that Karl Johan was able to push through his demands.

The result was that Frederik VI had to give up Norway to Sweden when the Treaty of Kiel was concluded in January 1814. Some time passed before the news reached Christian Frederik, but he had already decided that he would lead a revolt with the purpose of bringing about Norway's independence. The odds did not appear entirely hopeless, as by this point, Karl Johan had made himself internationally unpopular; and while Frederik VI did not encourage a Norwegian revolt, he did not take action to prevent one either, and he made sure that Norway received plentiful grain shipments.

Due to diplomatic considerations, Karl Johan gave up his demand that Norway should become a part of Sweden and modified his demand to the effect that Norway should become a party to a so-called personal union under the Swedish crown. In contrast, Christian Frederik insisted that the Norwegians did not wish to "become Swedish."

The Constitution of Norway

After having received news of the Treaty of Kiel, Christian Frederik considered immediately having himself proclaimed King of Norway, but he chose first to defy the Norwegian winter by travelling around the country to win people for the struggle for independence. On 19 February, however, he sent out an open letter encouraging people to fight for Norway accompanied by a proclamation in which he titled himself the "regent" of the Norwegian realm, assigning to himself the authority Frederik VI had given up. Thus, Christian Frederik took for himself the provisional status of an absolute monarch in accordance with the Royal Law.

The documents were published at Christiania on 22 February to great rejoicing. On the same occasion, it was made known that there would be elections with the purpose of selecting the members of a national assembly that would produce a constitution. The voting was to be carried out after church services around the country, and Christian Frederik had come up with the idea that the churchgoers should swear to stake their lives in a fight for Norway's independence. This was an effective way of creating emotional ties between the populace and the policy of pursuing independence, and Christian Frederik generally received

Christian Frederik's
declaration of ab-
dication. In the first
version, Christian
Frederik had only
given up the throne
on his own behalf,
but not on behalf
of his descendants.
This was done quite
consciously for the
Swedes had not
presented an explic-
it demand that he
give up the throne
on behalf of his de-
scendants, but at
the last moment,
he was forced to in-
clude his descend-
ants in the decla-
ration.

invaluable help from the Norwegian pulpits in connection with promoting his point of view. Furthermore, he was ahead of his time as regards actual news propaganda, as he made sure the Norwegian newspapers were given good advice with regard to what they should write.

Already on 24 February, two Swedish emissaries came to demand that Christian Frederik leave the country, but this demand was rejected on the grounds that Christian Frederik was remaining in the country in accordance with the will of the people. However, there were also other considerations, and the big question was whether it would be possible to get the great powers to support Norway's bid for independence. British support in particular would be decisive, so Christian Frederik wrote numerous letters to England and sent his friend Carsten Anker there as a diplomat.

On 10 April 1814, the national assembly that was to produce the constitution met at Eidsvoll to begin negotiations regarding Norway's first constitution. Not everyone in the assembly supported the policy of seeking independence—or wanted the strong monarchy desired by Christian Frederik—but the text of the constitution was ready after only six weeks of negotiations. Christian Frederik pretended to stay out of the negotiations but pulled the strings behind the scenes and made his mark on most aspects of the constitution. While the Eidsvoll constitution was one of Europe's most democratic, it accorded a significant amount of latitude to the monarchy.

On 17 May, the constitution was approved, and Christian Frederik was formally elected King of Norway. The following day, the assembly approved a formal letter to Sweden appealing for "friendship and association," while the great powers were called upon to prevent the oppression of the Norwegian people, who were "determined to choose death rather than the chains of slavery." On 19 May, Christian Frederik swore the royal oath that is called for by the constitution and still used by Norwegian kings; and on 22 May, he entered Christiania as King while the populace wept tears of joy.

The Swedish-Norwegian War
The hangovers came quickly, for the great powers' reactions to the Norwegian revolt were not encouraging. The British government felt bound by its agreements with Karl Johan, and when he returned to Sweden with his army in late May, the stage was set for war.

Erklæring!

Alene til Folkets Held har jeg villet bære Norges Krone. — Rigets nuværende Tilstand, Europas forenede Villie mod Norge, og Folket af, alle de Midler, der krævedes til at forsvare Norges Uafhængighed ikke ere tilstrækkelige for mine redelige Hensigter, endelig mit ved Kampens tilstundende Afslutning givne Løfte bevæger mig til at nedlegge Norges Krone tilligemed den udøvende Magt uden Forbeholdenhed, i Folkets Hænder for mig og Afkom. —

Jeg løser altsaa det norske Folk fra sin Troskabs-Eed til mig, og i hvor smerteligt det end maae være for mig at forlade et Folk, som jeg elsker og som har givet mig saa uforglemmelige Prøver paa sin Hengivenhed, saa bringer jeg dog dette Offer for at afværge Ulykker fra Fædrelandet. Betrygget ved Constitutionen, som Folket selv har givet sig, vil det norske Folks Selvstændighed og Frihed ikke forgaae, men lykkeligere Dage, det give Gud! opnaaes ved Fredens Velsignelser.

Ladegaardsøen den tiende October, Aar efter Christi Byrd Et tusind otte hundrede og fjorten. —

Christian Frederik

The situation represented a serious threat to Denmark for many tended to place the responsibility for the Norwegian revolt in Copenhagen. Therefore, Frederik VI needed to eradicate any suspicion that he was behind the revolt himself; and at this point, he had without a doubt become irritated—if not angered—by his cousin's behaviour. Christian Frederik had consistently failed to comply with his royal orders, and in the ears of Frederik VI, constitution was practically an expletive.

For his part, Norway's new king had to recognize the fact that the prospects for a future for his reign were hopeless, but he saw an opportunity to save the Norwegian constitution. In early June, a common deputation from the great powers (an Austrian, a Prussian, a Russian, and an Englishman) arrived to demand that the terms of the treaty be fulfilled, and it says a great deal about Christian Frederik's powers of persuasion that he managed to turn this into a winning situation in the course of a few days. The four delegates ended up formulating a mediation proposal that constituted de facto recognition of the Eidsvoll constitution, and Karl Johan was not accommodating when it was presented to him. The Swedish Crown Prince needed to secure the Swedish throne for himself and his line with a military victory, and on 26 July, he gave orders to attack.

The Swedish forces were superior with regard to numbers, material, and combat experience; and despite all of his advantageous qualities, Christian Frederik was no field commander. Rather, he was a man who would do what was necessary to avoid unnecessary loss of life, and he succeeded in achieving his most important goals with only a modest loss of human life. After some weeks of fighting characterized by Norwegian efforts that were largely defensive in nature, a peace treaty was arrived at on 13 August in Moss. As expected, Christian Frederik had to give up the Norwegian crown, but the constitution was, to a large extent, recognized, though it had to be rewritten and adapted in accordance with a union with Sweden.

Karl Johan's abstention from a total subjugation of Norway was probably due to the great powers' negative reactions to the war; in any event, he had got the victory he had wanted. He had secured his position as the successor to the Swedish throne, and—not least—he had managed to remove the halo from Christian Frederik, who was now made the scapegoat for the weak and uncertain defensive efforts that had caused a widespread feeling of shame in Norway. The departing King had to accept being portrayed as a weakling who couldn't stand the sight of blood.

As King of Norway, Christian Frederik appointed eighteen chamberlains, each of whom received a chamberlain's key like this one, which belonged to the councillor (konferensråd), Carl Henrik von Holten. The initials C. F. R. stand for Christian Frederik Rex.

Immediately after the conclusion of the peace treaty, half a year of inhuman pressure took its toll on Christian Frederik when he suffered a complete nervous breakdown. He isolated himself on the Bygdø peninsula near Oslo and stayed in bed for a time but did what he could to influence the rewriting of the constituti- on that was ongoing while he was recuperating. On 8 October, a deputation from the Storting arrived on Bygdø and received the King's declaration of abdication. After this, Christian Frederik said a teary farewell to the court, his staff, and the politicians who had appeared; and after a journey home that was long delayed by wind conditions, he was able to go ashore at Aarhus on 4 November 1814.

Home again

The political winds in Europe were not favourable for a rebellious prince who had been the godfather of a liberal constitution. Napoleon had been banished to Saint Helena, and Frederik VI had travelled to the Vienna congress, where an at- tempt was made to reestablish old power structures in the wake of the revolu- tionary wars. In this situation, Christian Frederik had to expect that he would be met with scepticism by the Danish elite.

However, the Jutlanders gave him a surprisingly warm reception. Princess Charlotte Frederikke also took the opportunity to make the journey from her exi- le in Horsens to Aarhus to convince her ex-spouse to resume their relationship, but Christian Frederik declined. In fact, he was on his way to Als to propose to Princess Caroline Amalie, who was the daughter of the late Duke Frederik of Augustenburg and Frederik VI's sister Duchess Louise Augusta of Augustenburg. During a visit to Augustenburg prior to his departure for Norway, he had taken an interest in the princess, who in the meantime had reached the age of eigh- teen and was therewith able to marry. Christian Frederik's diaries clearly show what his motivations were in this regard. His recent time in Norway had been lonely, and in this situation, he had come to long for a stable family life and had become determined to "become virtuous." He never succeeded in this, but the pair became engaged and was married in a simple ceremony at Augustenburg on 15 May 1815.

Christian Frederik did not avoid his punishment, however, for when Frederik VI had returned from Vienna, the King created an entirely superfluous post for his

After the loss of Norway, Odense Palace was made a governor's residence for Christian Frederik and Caroline Amalie. Their presence is supposed to have been responsible for the fact that Odense started to be called Little Copenhagen, and with the passage of years, Caroline Amalie in particular became popular in the town, thanks to her social projects. The statue in front of the building represents not Christian VIII but his son, Frederik VII, with the June constitution of 1849 in his hand.

cousin as governor of Funen with a residence in Odense. This constituted de fac-to exile, but the prince threw himself into his work with his usual energy, and in the following years, he increased the efficiency of work processes on Funen to the extent possible.

In the trivial provincial world in which he now found himself, Christian Frederik had to seek refuge in science and art, which he continued to do for many years to come. Since he had been a child, he had collected things, including minerals and insects; and during his long period of partial unemployment, Christian Frederik also became a passionate collector of conch shells, coins, medals from the revolutionary wars, and not least antique vases.

On 12 May 1817, Christian Frederik was also admitted to the freemasons' lodge Maria til de tre Hjerter ("Maria of the Three Hearts") in Odense as member number 122. Other central personages in his life such as Frederik VI and Bertel Thorvaldsen were also freemasons, but it is difficult for an outsider to evaluate how great a role this played in their lives or what they got out of it. As a good member of the brotherhood, Christian Frederik did not make reference to freemasonry in his notes and diaries, but he rose through the ranks, and in 1836, he replaced Prince Karl of Hesse-Kassel as Grandmaster of the Danish Order of Freemasons.

The journeys abroad

During the summer of 1818, Christian Frederik succeeded in securing approval for a journey with the justification that Caroline Amalie's health required a stay at a spa in Germany. The purpose of the journey, however, was to visit prominent European princes and smooth over any misunderstandings with regard to what had happened in Norway. During the journey, Christian Frederik was able to meet with the Russian and Austrian emperors as well as the most prominent European politician of the age, Prince Metternich, who became a role model for Christian Frederik.

Christian Frederik's wanderlust was not satisfied by the first journey, however, so the Prince planned a longer journey the following winter that practically became a traditional Grand Tour, but one undertaken at a more mature age than was usual. Christian Frederik took care to include all the cities, landsca-

Caroline Amalie's notebook was decorated with this little painting of the view of the Quisisana Palace near Naples, which was the palace that was put at the disposal of the Prince and Princess during the summer and fall of 1820. It was almost certainly painted by J. C. Dahl, a Norwegian who was a guest of the art-loving Danish couple for several months and later became world famous. It was Christian Frederik who persuaded the painter to come to Italy, and they remained in contact throughout Christian Frederik's life. The Prince purchased works of art and promoted the artist's work in Denmark.

pes, museums, and scholarly societies that could interest him, and the journey began with an extensive tour of Germany and continued to Switzerland and Austria before reaching the primary goal of the prince's cultural pilgrimage: Italy.

Around Christmas 1819, Christian Frederik and Caroline Amalie arrived in Rome, where they let themselves be intoxicated by the highlights of the city before they proceeded to Naples, where they ended up staying most of the year. Ferdinand I, who was King of the Two Sicilies (Naples/Sicily), was generous with dinners and hunting outings, and Christian Frederik climbed Mount Vesuvius, where he made mineralogical observations—his main hobby—after which he lectured on his findings. After another stay in Rome, a palace outside Naples was placed at their disposal, and many social events took place there.

As the couple's luck would have it, however, a revolution broke out in 1820. This was one of many revolts in the Mediterranean region, where people had been inspired by Spain and were demanding liberal reforms, so Naples and Sicily im-

During his stay in Naples in 1820, Christian Frederik developed what would be a life-long interest in antique vases, and he bought a fine collection from the Archbishop of Naples. The collection included this mixing vessel for wine and water, which was found in the city of Bari in Southern Italy. Today, Christian Frederik's collections of antiques, coins, and medals constitute the nucleus of the collection of Classical and Near Eastern Antiquities and the Royal Collection of Coins and Medals at the National Museum.

plemented constitutions, and royal power became subordinate to a parliament. Christian Frederik found this transformation radical himself, but the very fact that he was in the city made the leader of the Norwegian revolt an even more suspicious figure. Soon after this, the great powers reacted to the revolts with military intervention, and the Danish couple and their circle wisely chose to depart in December 1820.

After he had returned to Rome, Christian Frederik realized his long-standing wish to meet the sculptor Bertel Thorvaldsen. In the time that followed, they saw each other often, while as usual, the prince filled his days with as much art, culture, and science as possible. In fact, the two men became such good friends that Thorvaldsen loaned Christian Frederik what was at the time a stagge-

Caroline Amalie portrayed by Marie Marguerite. On the back, the model herself has written: "This portrait of me was painted in Plombières in the year 1821 when Christian made the dangerous journey in Switzerland via Grumzel [?] and Furka . I gave this portrait to Christian the same year as a birthday present. It was mounted in a portfolio. Caroline Amalie."

During their first stay in Rome, the successor to the Danish throne and his wife visited Bertel Thorvaldsen's workshop, where Christian Frederik ordered ten miniatures of the artist's statues (and one by his assistant) in gilded bronze. They were to be used in a spectacular table decoration, and during his onward journey, the Prince ordered candelabras, plateau mirrors, and centrepieces in Paris. The table decoration can be seen on the bel étage in Christian VIII's Palace, where the items are displayed in accordance with the original plan.

ring sum of money. An ability to balance his private economy was not one of the Prince's many positive qualities, and his debt to Thorvaldsen was not the only one he had difficulty repaying.

In the context of the revolutionary fever sweeping through Southern Italy, Rome also became an unsafe place to be. So in March 1821, the Danish company travelled via Switzerland to France, where rumours about Christian Frederik's revolutionary engagement were already circulating. This was worrying and necessitated a diplomatic charm offensive, but after doing a great deal of groundwork, Christian Frederik succeeded in convincing the Russian envoy that he was a true aristocrat. This was talked about in the salons of Paris, and he and Caroline Amalie were subsequently welcomed everywhere. In May, they took their leave of the French king and travelled on to England, where they spent a few months in the company of politicians, artists, and royalty before Frederik VI called them home. The journeys had cost more than enough.

On the sidelines

After they had returned home in September 1821, Christian Frederik and Caroline Amalie were permitted to stay in the capital city—in the palace at Amalienborg and at Sorgenfri Palace—to the extent that the governor's post on Funen allowed it. However, Frederik VI did not wish to involve his cousins in matters of government, and it was not until 1831 that he was given a seat on the Council of State. Even then, the members of the council followed Frederik VI's example by turning a deaf ear to Christian Frederik's speeches.

All the evidence suggests that the reasons for this were political rather than personal, for the King and the successor to the throne appear to have had an excellent relationship privately. They established closer ties when, in 1828, Prince Frederik (VII) married the King's youngest daughter, Princess Vilhelmine, in connection with which the old family dispute was to be set aside. However, the marriage turned into a catastrophe and was annulled in 1834, after which the drunken Prince Frederik was banished to Fredericia.

The wave of revolutions that rolled through Europe in 1830 was scarcely noticed in Denmark. However, a political innovation in the form of the advisory as-

Full-length portraits of Caroline Amalie and Christian Frederik painted by Louis Aumont in 1830 and in 1831, respectively. Caroline Amalie is portrayed together with the marble version of Thorvaldsen's bust of her husband in Roman attire. Today, this bust is in the office of the Norwegian Prime Minister in Oslo.

The Hans Christian Andersen monument in the King's Garden. Some believe that H. C. Andersen was actually the son of Christian VIII and Countess Elise Ahlefeldt Laurvig, who are supposed to have met in Germany in 1804. This notion has been presented as an explanation of the many favours that helped the author achieve fame. To be sure, it is well known that Christian VIII and Caroline Amalie were fond of H. C. Andersen—and he of them—and frequently invited him to visit them, but it is still the dominant view that the author's unusual success in social life is to be attributed to his ability to entertain.

semblies of the estates of the realm was introduced the following year. These assemblies first met in 1835. The Royal Law was still in effect, but despite the fact that they had only an advisory function, these assemblies played a role in paving the way for the democracy that was to come because they provided people with an opportunity to exercise political influence.

As a member of the Council of State, Christian Frederik, who was always well prepared, attempted to implement a series of initiatives but did not achieve

N.F.S. Grundtvig (1783-1872)

much. One of his trademark projects was freedom of the press—he was a per-
sistent advocate for reducing censorship—and he did his best to push prac-
tices in the criminal justice system in a more humane direction. In reality, however, the prince was able to exercise almost no influence until he succeeded
to the throne in 1839, and he had to apply his energy to other pursuits. He was
constantly occupied by books and his growing collections, and one could expect to meet him at the theatre, at concerts, and at art exhibitions. He corre-
sponded extensively with foreign scientists and intellectuals, and he had great

knowledge and an assured taste as an art connoisseur. At home in Denmark, he discussed the natural sciences with H. C. Ørsted, architecture with C. F. Hansen, literature with Adam Oehlenschläger and Jens Baggesen, and art with C. W. Eckersberg, and he got to know everyone in Denmark who excelled in some artistic or intellectual endeavour.

When Frederik VI became seriously ill in 1837, it looked as though there would be a change of King, but the old king made a fairly complete recovery. The following year, Christian Frederik journeyed abroad with the intention of finding a wife for his unruly son but with the equally important purpose of meeting with top European leaders as diplomatic preparation for his coming time as King. Denmark was a small but strategically important country that constantly had to take the interests of the great powers into consideration. Once again the Prince received important advice from Prince Metternich, who, on the occasion of the Prince's visit to Bad Gastein, emphasized the importance of "resolutely acting to uphold basic conservative principles," as the prince put it in his diary.

After Christian Frederik had returned home, almost a year passed during which the country was practically paralysed by a weakened king. But on 3 December 1839, Frederik VI died, and it was proclaimed from the balcony at Amalienborg that Denmark's King was now called Christian VIII.

The last of the absolute monarchs

As Denmark's new king, Christian VIII faced a challenge that was entirely different from the one he had faced in Norway. While in Norway his task had been to ensure the independence of a relatively unified nation, he now had to navigate in a country characterized by major political disputes and do so in a way that would be approved of by the great powers.

Unmet expectations

The early part of Christian VIII's reign presented difficulties precisely because of the King's past actions in Norway. He was immediately confronted with the demand that Denmark be given a democratic constitution, and the country's liberal forces were bitterly disappointed when this did not occur. This was perceived as evidence that the passage of years had rendered him weak and incapable of

44   Christian VIII.

taking initiative, but it would have been impossible for Christian VIII to have lived up to liberal expectations. Consideration for the possible reactions of the great powers was decisive, for eagerness to bring about social reforms was evident in many parts of Europe, and no one was interested in having Denmark set a progressive example.

What was most disappointing to the liberal powers—and reassuring to the foreign envoys—was probably that Christian VIII chose to keep Frederik VI's aging ministers, though it turned out that he would seldom follow their commandments. His purpose was not least to win the trust of government administrators and conservatives, whom the King needed to have on his side if a reform programme was to succeed.

If anyone had experienced the weaknesses of the absolute monarchy, it was Christian VIII, and he understood that it would be impossible to maintain in the long run, but he could only pave the way by means of gradual reforms. He responded to the often-heard references to the Eidsvoll constitution by saying that it had been "work done in haste"—by which he meant that the transition to a constitutional monarchy should not be characterized by hasty work this time. Naturally, this way of putting things did not make him popular in Norway, where the constitution was already regarded as a national treasure.

Early in his reign, Christian VIII implemented a reform of local government that went a good deal farther in the direction of local self-government than Frederik VI would have accepted, and in 1841, he followed up with the national local government law, which introduced regional councils and was thus a further step in the same direction. He also made a significant contribution to getting the state's finances under control by creating an agency responsible for economic administration, and it was decided that starting 1841, annual government budgets would be published, which was an important step toward a more transparent administration.

The Danish network of roads was greatly improved, farmers' duty to work on road building and maintenance was abolished, and in 1842, a long-needed reform of the army was implemented. As expected, Christian VIII also implemented reforms of the criminal justice system: Corporal punishment was largely abolished, prison sentences were shortened, and the use of torture during inter-

On 28 June 1840, Christian VIII was anointed in Frederiksborg Castle Chapel with all the ceremonials that had characterized royal anointments since the introduction of absolute monarchy. This was the last anointment of a king in Danish history, and at this point, it seemed dramatically out of step with the times, but the new King preferred to maintain the old rituals. The drawing shows a number of intellectual guests of honour such as H. C. Andersen, N. F. S. Grundtvig, Adam Oehlenschläger, and H.C. Ørsted. Attempts to persuade the somewhat-wilful Bertel Thorvaldsen to attend were not successful.

Christian VIII's cor-
onation procession
in the Frederiksborg
Castle courtyard.
Detail of the paint-
ing by Johan Vilhelm
Gertner, 1840.

rogations was abolished. Military penal laws became less harsh, and while the time was not yet ripe for the abolition of death penalty, Christian VIII typically made an effort to get persons who had been sentenced to death pardoned. Another of Christian VIII's trademark projects was bringing about the freeing of the slaves in the Danish West Indies, and in 1848, he succeeded in this. With regard to freedom of the press, Christian VIII's declarations of intent appeared to reflect the views of his predecessor, but in practice, the King changed course completely. Frederik VI frequently brought charges in order to thwart what he called "the audacity of writers," while Christian VIII refrained from interfering, though he did support those press organs from which he could expect support himself.

The reforms were implemented as a result of the King's own initiative, and he took upon himself the responsibility imposed on him by the absolute monarchy system by going over huge amounts of material himself. Nevertheless, Christian VIII found time for a steady stream of audiences, for the change of King gave people new hope that their concerns would be listened to. It was generally known that Christian VIII, in contrast to his predecessor, was a man one could talk to.

The Schleswig problem

The question of the constitution was quickly trumped by the national conflict created by Danish-German tensions in the duchies. Already in May of 1840, the King intervened in the sensitive question of language in Schleswig by ordering that Danish be used by public authorities in Danish-speaking areas. All that was actually intended was that both languages should be used in parallel, but Christian VIII had stuck his hand into a wasp's nest. The German nationalistic movement in Schleswig-Holstein was growing in strength, and the so-called language rescript provided a reason for further mobilization. The Duke of Augustenburg, Queen Caroline Amalie's brother, started a heated press campaign that made him the standard-bearer of anti-Copenhagen policies. He believed he had the right to inherit the duchies if the Danish monarchy's male line became extinct, and while the German nationalistic movement desired a free constitution most of all, there was agreement that the monarchy should be resisted. It helped not a bit that as a gesture of reconciliation, Christian VIII appointed the Duke's younger brother, the Prince of Noer, governor of Schleswig-Holstein in 1842.

After the anointment, the King and Queen undertook a major tour of the Danish market towns. During this tour, as Christian VIII had foreseen, they encountered none of the hostility that was evident in Copenhagen. Political resistance to absolute monarchy was a big-city phenomenon that had not reached the broad populace. Illustration by P. C. Klæstrup, ca. 1875.

The mature Christian VIII painted by Wilhelm Marstrand in 1843. The King bears the star of the Order of the Elephant and a many-coloured ribbon in his buttonhole. It is not known what document is represented in the picture.

However, not only those sympathetic to the German side were mobilized by the language issue. Six thousand people assembled in 1843 at the first public meeting on Skamlingsbanken to celebrate the language rescript, which was immediately followed by an only slightly smaller public festival at Aabenraa for the German nationalistic movement. When, in 1844, Christian VIII followed up with the so-called "language patent," which formulated a compromise with regard to the right to use Danish in the Schleswig assembly, this only made both sides even more combative despite the fact that the opposite effect had been intended.

The prize at stake in this conflict was Schleswig, which one side wanted to be German, the other Danish. The national liberals in Denmark, who were led by Orla Lehmann, felt that Holstein and Lauenburg should be given up and that Schleswig should be incorporated into Denmark. The Augustenburgers maintained that they had a right of inheritance with regard to both duchies, which the German nationalistic movement wanted to turn into a German state. Christian VIII, on the other hand, felt obliged to maintain the conglomerate state for which he had been made responsible and felt no understanding for the new militant nationalism. The King could not accommodate either of the parties without angering the other, and this was a difficult situation in which to manoeuvre for a man who loved applause.

The national question constituted a significant obstacle to the production of a constitution establishing a real division of power between the King and elected officials. The smallest step in that direction could become a bomb under the common governmental structure that bound the duchies and the kingdom together, and a common constitution was a surefire recipe for unrest.

The succession

When he took his place on the Danish throne, Christian VIII faced a special problem that was closely associated with the national question and that he did not succeed in solving. The problem was that there was a lack of a successor to the throne who could follow his son, Prince Frederik. Briefly, there was hope that an heir might be born after a new marriage was arranged for Prince Frederik. In 1841, he married Princess Mariane of Mecklenburg-Strelitz. But after a few years, she had had enough of her husband's bad habits and returned home.

However, the Royal Law contained an obvious solution to the problem of the succession. It contained a rule to the effect that the line of succession should continue via the closest female relation if the last direct successor died without sons. Christian VIII's sister Charlotte had a son, Prince Friedrich, and when Christian VIII succeeded in getting him married to a daughter of the Russian tsar in 1844, a solution the Augustenburgers would have to accept appeared to have been found. The joy was short-lived, however, for she died after half a year of marriage, which rendered the succession question more open.

The big question was whether the Royal Law applied to the duchies, and in 1846, tensions reached a level that caused Christian to take decisive action. On 8 July, he published his famous "open letter," which had been signed by the Council of State and maintained that the succession rules of the Royal Law applied to Denmark and Schleswig, while there was a need for clarification with regard to parts of Holstein. The reactions in the duchies were violent. Censorship had to be increased due to the hot-headed agitation, and many government officials resigned in protest. While the open letter increased tensions, it was positively received in Denmark, and it increased respect for the King, which was not a small gain.

When this storm had died down, there was a calmer period in Denmark and the duchies. This allowed Christian VIII to proceed with the preparation of a constitution, and he initiated a series of studies in order to be able to structure the future constitutional state apparatus as soon as possible. As had been the case in Norway, one of the primary goals was securing the balance of power between the parliament and the executive royal power as the main axis of a constitutional monarchy system. Christian VIII appears to have been aiming for a deadline in September 1848 when the Oldenburg line would celebrate the 400th anniversary of its first king's accession to the Danish throne—a perfect occasion for a magnificent gesture such as the proclamation of a new constitution. But while this would have been the high point of his reign, the King had reason for concern; he knew that a constitution should be introduced before a change of King, as his son was not capable of confronting this task, and he knew that it was very likely to cause a crisis.

Christian VIII did not make it. In early January 1848, he contracted a cold when he said farewell to the crew of the corvette Valkyrie, who were embarking on an expedition. He was treated by being bled—this was the dubious standard treatment method of the day—and got blood poisoning in the process. His condition went downhill rapidly, and on 17 January, the King was carried into his vase cabinet to die with his beloved collection around him. Three days later, on 20 January 1848, Christian VIII died. As his last will, he left to his son a letter commanding him to proclaim a law implementing a common constitution for Denmark and the duchies upon his accession to the throne.

Drawing of Christian VIII in his relatively modest study in the palace at Amalienborg. When this drawing was executed, the King had been dead for many years. But on the basis of other portraits, he was drawn into the room, which still appeared as it had in his time. Drawn in 1883 by Christian Hetsch, who copied a lithograph by A. Juul and E. Fortling from the 1860s.

The legacy

Christian VIII died at the beginning of the year of revolutions, 1848, and precisely two months after his death, the so-called Casino Meeting was held. After which, the government resigned and Frederik VII declared that he viewed the absolute monarchy as terminated and himself as a constitutional king. This constituted the starting shot of the First Schleswig War, which ended up confirming status quo but at least resulted in a solution to the problem of the succession as Prince Christian (IX) of Glücksburg was designated successor after the war.

Christian VIII lying
in state, painted by
Niels Simonsen,
1848.

Photograph of Queen Dowager Caroline Amalie signed by Georg E. Hansen in 1873. Because of her long widowhood, Caroline Amalie practically ended up enjoying greater prestige than her husband had. Her projects included the establishment of children's homes; she was a driving force behind the creation of the foundation Diakonissestiftelsen in Denmark. Above all, the Queen Dowager represented continuity, which was important for the monarchy during these years in which the constituted created new conditions and a new branch of the family took over when Christian IX became King.

One could say that Christian VIII died too early to be remembered. All over Denmark there are statues of "the giver of the constitution," Frederik VII, while his father went down in Danish history as a representative of the scrapped absolute monarchy, and his legacy was marked by the unmet liberal expectations.

It is worth considering what Christian VIII's reign might have been like if Frederik VI had died ten years earlier, for his many years on the sidelines certainly did not strengthen Christian VIII. There are many testimonials from contemporaries to the effect that despite his unsurpassed eloquence, he had difficulty breaking through to people and getting them to respect him as King, and this characte-

During the first months of 1821, when Christian Frederik and Caroline Amalie had the pleasure of Bertel Thorvaldsen's company in Rome, the sculptor modelled these busts, which are cast in bronze.

rization seems to be supported by the words of one of his acquaintances, the philosopher Søren Kierkegaard. After the King's death, Kierkegaard wrote that "Christian VIII was a man of brilliant talents but actually lost in his great wisdom, which lacked a corresponding and proportional moral background."

In Norway, Christian Frederik ended up with a legacy that was downright unjust. As the man responsible for the deficient defences during the Swedish-Norwegian War, he was long portrayed as a weak and superficial individual who had blown himself up to a saviour figure and then run away with his tail between his legs. In the long run, however, there was no ignoring the importance of the role played by Christian Frederik in the creation and defence of the constitution Norwegians celebrate on 17 May, and with the passage of years, he has been accorded honour and dignity in Norwegian historiography.

Women have not taken up as much space in this little book about Christian VIII as they did in his life. But while the mistresses of kings were known to the public in earlier times, Christian VIII was discreet in connection with his affairs, so they are not actually essential elements to his story. However, he was survived by other children than Frederik VII. In Norway, his mistress Marie Eide bore him a son, Frederik Carl Eide, and in the course of many years, Frederik, Frederikke, and Fanny were borne to him by Sophie Frederikke Kraft, the mistress with whom he had the longest-lasting relationship. In accordance with the royal line's long-standing tradition, Christian VIII took care of his extramarital children, and they visited him often.

We do not know what Queen Caroline Amalie thought about these matters, but she is unlikely to have been ignorant of the King's affairs. We do know, however, that she did not take her husband's death very hard but rather enjoyed her long period of widowhood greatly. She survived Christian VIII by more than thirty years and became an institution both in the royal family and in Copenhagen intellectual life. She carried out tireless charity work, and until her death in 1881, the greatest cultural personalities of the age continued to stream to the palace at Amalienborg, which is now called Christian VIII's Palace.